Christmas activities

Ray Gibson and Fiona Watt

Designed by Joe Pedley
Illustrated by Amanda Barlow
Photographs by Howard Allman

Additional illustrations by Chris Chaisty, Michaela Kennard, Mikki Rain and Sue Stitt
Additional photography by Ray Moller

SCHOLASTIC INC.
New York Toronto London Auckland Sydney
Mexico City New Delhi Hong Kong

Christmas stockings

1. Fold a piece of paper as large as this page, in half, like this.

2. Use a pencil to draw a stocking shape on the front.

3. Cut out the stocking, but don't cut along the folded edge.

Roll little pieces of tissue paper into balls and glue them on.

Draw shapes with glue and sprinkle on lots of glitter, or glitter glue.

Tape on a loop of thread and hang the stockings on your Christmas tree.

Don't glue along the top.

4. Open the stocking Glue around one side, then fold the front over.

5. Rub your hand over the part you glued to flatten it.

6. Decorate your stocking using stickers, glitter and pens.

You could put a candy stick or a small chocolate bar inside each stocking.

You could decorate a stocking with stickers from the sticker pages in this book.

Paper cutouts

1. Cut out a circle from paper. Crayon all over one side of it.

2. Fold the circle in half, and then fold it in half again.

3. Cut out different shapes from around the edges.

4. Open the circle and flatten it. Tape a piece of thread on the back.

Other ideas

You could start with a square of paper instead of a circle.

Add some sparkle with spots of glue, then sprinkle on some glitter.

Use bright wrapping paper or paper from magazines.

Make lots of decorations using different-sized shapes.

These decorations look a little like snowflakes if you make them from white paper.

5

Snowman paperchain

1. Lay two pieces of thin paper with their short sides together. Join them with tape.

2. Fold the paper in half. Then, fold it again so that you get a zigzag shape.

3. Draw a snowman's hat at the top of the paper. Draw a head below the hat.

Don't cut the along the folds.

4. Draw a band all the way across the paper. This will be the snowman's arms.

5. Add a big, round tummy. Draw in some fat legs. Add two feet to the legs.

6. Draw around the shape with a felt-tip pen. Cut it out along these lines.

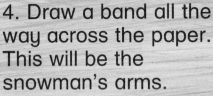

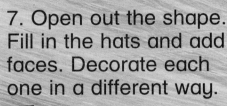

7. Open out the shape. Fill in the hats and add faces. Decorate each one in a different way.

You can join your snowmen into one long chain and hang them up.

Glittering shapes

1. Press a big cookie cutter firmly into a slice of white bread.

2. Push the bread shape out of the cutter very carefully.

3. Press the end of a straw into the shape to make a hole.

4. Put the bread shape onto a baking rack. Leave it overnight. It will go hard.

5. Mix a little paint with household glue (PVA). Paint around the edges of the shape.

6. Paint the top of the shape. When it is dry, turn it over and paint the other side.

7. Glue lots of glitter onto the top of the shape. Add sequins and tiny beads, too.

8. Push a long piece of thread through the hole. Make a loop at the end of the thread.

9. Push the ends of the thread through the loop. Make a knot and pull it tight.

Make lots of
decorations using
different shapes of
cookie cutters.

Hang these on your
Christmas tree or use
them as hanging
decorations.

These bread shapes are
for decoration only.
Do not eat them.

9

Christmas trees

Press on
stickers from
the sticker
pages.

Sprinkle
glitter onto
wet paint
or glue.

Print stars in
gold paint
(see page 16).

Press on
shiny star
stickers.
Add wavy
lines of
glitter.

Roll up pieces
of tissue paper
and glue them on.

10

1. Put a large, round object, such as a cake tin or dinnerplate, onto some thick paper.

2. Draw around it, then cut around the circle you have drawn. Fold the circle in half.

3. Open out the circle. Cut along the fold so that you have two semicircles of paper.

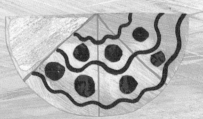

4. Fold one semicircle in half, then open it out. Make another tree with the other semicircle.

5. Fold one corner into the middle and crease it. Do the same with the other corner.

6. Open out each side then, turn the paper over and press it down to flatten it.

Don't decorate this end.

7. Decorate three parts with glitter, stickers, pens or paper shapes. Leave one end bare.

8. Carefully spread glue all over the part which you didn't deco-rate.

9. Fold the shape around and press it together to make a tree shape.

Christmas tree letters

For about eight letters, you will need:
125g (fi cup) plain flour
50g (⅟ cup) margarine
50g (⅟ cup) brown sugar
A small egg, beaten
1 teaspoon of ground ginger
A greased baking tray

Turn the oven to 190°C, 375°F, gas mark 5 before you begin.

1. Put the margarine and the sugar into a big bowl. Mix them well until they make a creamy mixture.

Sift the flour.

Add a little more flour if the dough feels very sticky.

Use a rolling pin.

2. Stir the mixture and add the egg a little at a time. Sift the flour and the ginger onto the mixture in the bowl.

3. Stir everything together to make a smooth mix. Squeeze it with your hands to make a firm dough.

4. Sprinkle flour onto a work surface and put the dough on it. Roll the dough until it is about 1cm (fiin) thick.

Use a blunt knife.

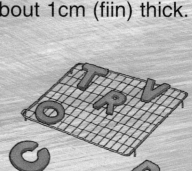

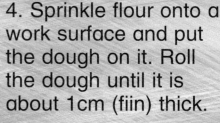

5. Cut out letter shapes. Squeeze all the scraps together and roll it again. Then, cut out more letters.

6. Use a spatula to lift each letter onto the greased tray. Bake the letters for about 15 minutes.

7. Ask for help to lift the baking tray out of the oven. Lift the letters onto a rack. Leave them to cool.

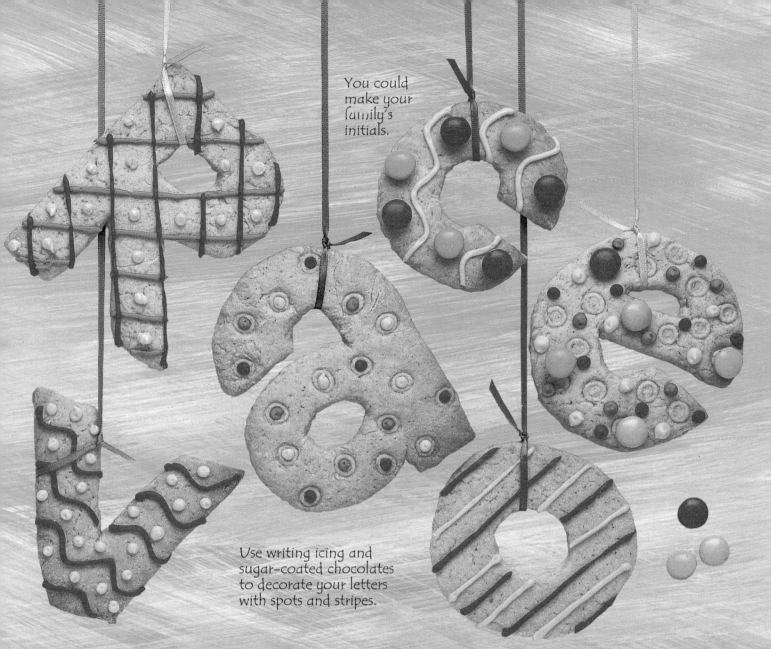

You could make your family's initials.

Use writing icing and sugar-coated chocolates to decorate your letters with spots and stripes.

Decorating ideas

Do this after your letters have cooled.

To make a spotted letter, press a large, clean pen top into the dough before you bake the letters.

When your letters have cooled, add patterns using writing icing. You can buy this in a supermarket.

When the letters are cooked, put a spot of icing on the back of a sugar-coated chocolate, then press it on a letter.

Gift tags
Stars

You could write a name in the middle of the star.

1. Press the sharp edge of a star-shaped cookie cutter into half a potato.

3. Before the paint dries, sprinkle it with lots of glitter. Shake off any extra glitter.

2. Press the star into some thick paint, then press it onto thin cardboard.

4. Cut around the star, a little way away from the glitter. Tape ribbon on the back.

Snowmen

Small end

You don't need the middle piece.

Big end

1. Cut the ends off a carrot, so that you have a big end and a small one.

2. Dip the big end into thick paint. Press it onto thin cardboard, for a body.

Use pens to draw the face, hat and buttons.

3. Print a head with the small end. When it's dry, draw on a face, hat and buttons.

Round tags

Put the paint on an old plate.

1. Dip the edge of a piece of cardboard into gold paint. Print a criss-cross pattern on thin cardboard.

2. When the paint is dry, put a small lid on the cardboard and draw around it. Cut out the circle.

3. Use felt-tip pens to decorate the circle. Draw stripes and zigzags. Tape ribbon on the back.

Try drawing different faces on the snowman tags.

Wrapping paper

1. You will need a cookie cutter and a potato, which is bigger than the cutter.

2. Cut a slice from the middle of the potato. Make it as thick as your thumb.

3. Push out the shape you have cut. You may need some help with the last two steps.

Try using gold or silver poster paint.

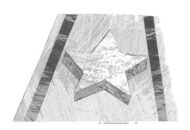

4. Dab both sides of the potato shape on some kitchen paper towels to dry it.

5. Press a fork into the shape. This will stop your hands getting too messy when you print.

6. Pour two or three small patches of paint onto newspaper. Do them close together.

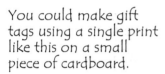

You could make gift tags using a single print like this on a small piece of cardboard.

7. Dip the shape into the middle of the paint, then press it onto a piece of paper.

8. Dip the shape into the paint again then print it. Fill the paper with printed shapes.

Use different shapes of cookie cutters together.

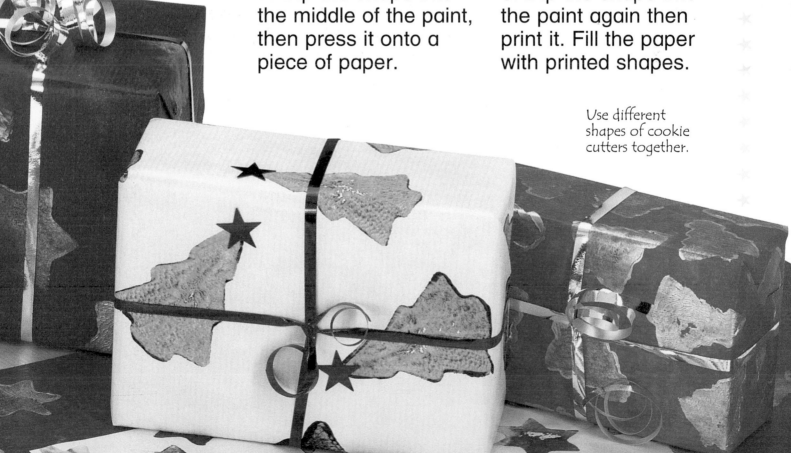

Christmas party snow queen

Attach the crown to your hair with hairpins.

You could paint wiggly blue lines on your face with face paints.

Use blue fabric for a cloak. Press on some snowflake sticker from the sticker pages.

Crown

Glue foil on the outside if the bottle isn't clear.

1. Cover the inside of a big (3l.) plastic bottle with glue. Press pieces of kitchen foil onto it.

2. Cut four pieces of foil as tall and wide as this book. Cut each piece in two from end to end.

3. Fold each piece of foil in half, like this. Squeeze each one into a long thin shape.

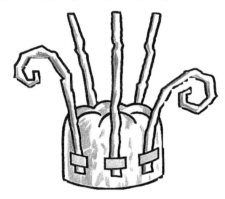

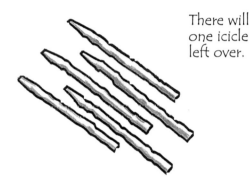

There will be one icicle left over.

4. Tape five of the pieces evenly around the side of the bottlle. Curl their ends over.

5. Cut the other pieces of foil in half. Pinch one end of each piece to make a pointed icicle.

6. Tape five of the icicles around the bottle, in between the long ones.

Wand

Ring

7. Tape a piece of foil around the bottom of the crown to hide all the ends.

Make a small cutout decoration like the ones on page 4. Glue it onto a stick.

To make a ring, wrap the spare icicle around a finger. Twist the end into a spiral.

Christmas treats

You will need:
70g (2fl oz.) digestive biscuits*
110g (4 oz.) icing or powdered sugar
25g (3 tablespoons or 1fl oz.) cocoa
50g (4 tablespoons) butter, melted
1 teaspoon of cinnamon or dissolved instant coffee
half a teaspoon of vanilla extract

Tie a rubber band around the bag.

1. Put the biscuits into a clean plastic bag. Use a rolling pin to crush them until they make fine crumbs.

2. Sift the sugar and cocoa into a big bowl. Use a wooden spoon to stir in the butter, coffee and vanillla.

These treats are the actual size to make each ball of mixture, at step 4.

The balls will take about half an hour to harden.

3. Pour the crumbs into the bowl. Mix them in. Then, use your hands to squeeze the mixture into a ball.

4. Break off pieces of the mixture and roll them into small balls. Make them about the size of walnuts.

5. Put the finished balls onto a large plate. Leave them in a cool place until they become firm.

*In US = Graham crackers

For logs, roll the mixture into a sausage shape. Use a fork to press lines in the top. Sprinkle them with a little icing or powdered sugar.

Decorating the treats

You will need:
4 tablespoons of icing or powdered sugar
cherries

The icing should just dribble off the spoon.

1. Mix small amounts of water with the sugar, a little at a time, until it is like thick glue.

2. Using a teaspoon, dribble a little icing carefully over the top of each ball.

3. Cut little pieces of cherry. Press a piece on top of each one, before the icing sets.

Christmas necklace

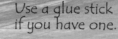

Use a glue stick if you have one.

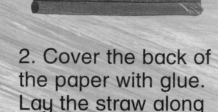

1. Cut a piece of wrapping paper as long as a fat straw. Make it the height of your little finger.

2. Cover the back of the paper with glue. Lay the straw along one edge, then roll it up tightly in the paper.

3. Cover more straws with wrapping paper. For a very long necklace you will need five straws.

4. When the glue is dry, cut the straws into different sizes of beads. Cut some long and some short.

5. Thread a blunt needle with strong thread. Tape the end of the thread to a work surface.

6. Thread on the beads until you have used them all. Tie the ends to make a necklace.

You could make long strings of beads to decorate your Christmas tree. Tie the thread around the last bead at each end.

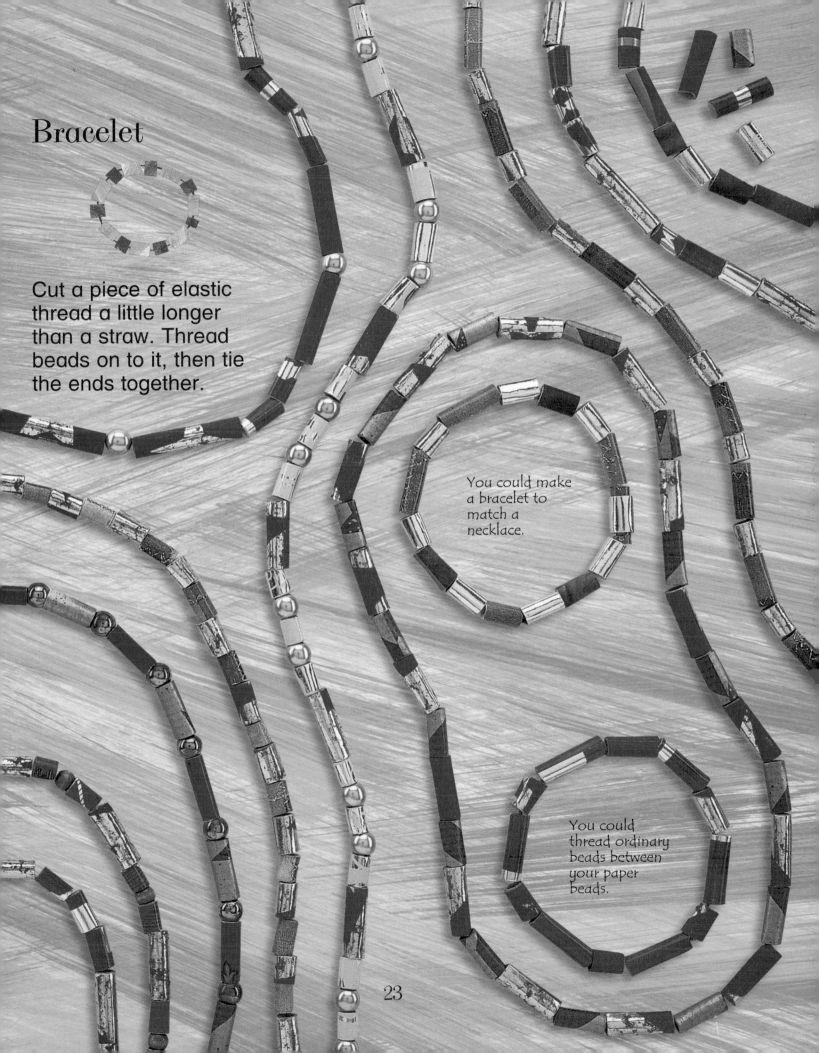

Bracelet

Cut a piece of elastic thread a little longer than a straw. Thread beads on to it, then tie the ends together.

You could make a bracelet to match a necklace.

You could thread ordinary beads between your paper beads.

23

Polar bear pop-up

The pieces of paper should be the same size.

Keep the paper folded as you cut.

   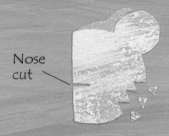

Nose cut

1. Fold a piece of white paper in half. Do the same with a piece of blue paper.

2. On the white paper, draw half of a bear's head against the fold, like this.

3. Cut around the head. Make a cut for a nose. Cut out shapes for fur, too.

The polar bear pops up in the middle of the card. You'll need to decorate the front too.

Follow the steps on page 14 for a glitter star.

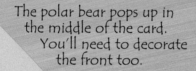 

4. Lift the nose and fold it flat onto the front, like this. Crease the fold. Fold it behind, too.

5. Open out the head. Push a finger through the nose from the back, so that it stands up.

Press on a sticker from the sticker pages.

Glue on a paper shape (see page 4). Dab on thick white paint for snow. Sprinkle it with sugar.

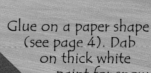 

6. Use felt-tip pens to draw a mouth and eyes. Carefully fill in the nose.

Match the middle folds.

7. Glue the back of the head, but not the nose. Press the head onto the blue paper.

Use paint and sugar for snow, see left.

8. Cut a rectangle of wrapping paper for a present. Glue it on below the head.

9. Cut two paws from white paper. Glue them on. Add claws with a black pen.

A reindeer

1. Use a crayon to draw the body. Add a neck.

2. Draw the head and add two ears.

3. Add four long legs and a tail.

4. Crayon hooves, a nose and two eyes.

5. Draw jagged antlers on its head.

6. Add spikes to the antlers. Fill in with pens.

To draw a fir tree

1. Draw the trunk of a tree with a crayon.

2. Add branches with a light green crayon.

3. Draw dark green branches over the top.

Glue your picture to a piece of stiff folded paper to make a Christmas card.

Printed penguins

1. Lay some kitchen paper towels onto a thick pile of old newspapers.

2. Pour some black paint on top. Spread the paint with the back of a spoon.

3. Cut a big potato in half. Then, cut away two sides, like this, to make a handle.

4. To print the body, press the potato into the paint then press it onto some paper.

5. When the paint has dried, use a smaller potato to print a white tummy on the penguin.

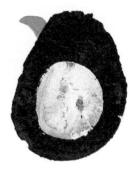

6. Dip a brush in a little orange paint and paint a pointed beak on the side of the penguin.

7. Use a brush to paint a curved black flipper on each side of the penguin's body.

8. For the penguin's feet, paint two orange triangles at the bottom of the body.

9. Paint a white eye. When the paint is dry, add a black dot to the middle of the eye.

Print your penguin
onto half a piece of
stiff paper. Fold it to
make a Christmas card.

29

A handprinted angel

This is an
upside-down
dress.

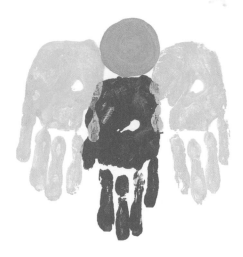

1. Press your hand in
blue paint, then press it
in the middle of a piece
of paper.

2. Press both hands
into yellow paint. Make
two prints a bit lower,
for the wings.

3. Turn your paper.
Dip your finger in pink
paint. Go around and
around, for a head.

4. Use your fingertip to
do blue arms. Join
them to the dress.
Add some hands.

5. Use orange paint to
finger paint some hair.
Add a yellow halo
above the head.

6. Dot on some eyes
and a nose. Use your
fingertip to paint a
smiling mouth.

Fingerpaint lots
of stars around
your angel.

Glue your angel
picture to a piece
of stiff paper to
make a large
Christmas card.

Fingerprint fat robins

You could print your
picture directly onto a
piece of folded stiff paper
to make a Christmas card.

Print them in
a line like this.

1. Dip the end of one finger in brown paint. Print it onto paper. Do three more prints.

2. Dip a finger into red paint and press it onto each brown shape for a tummy.

3. Fingerpaint a spot of white paint below the red one. Let them overlap.

4. Print a brown tail and black legs, using the edge of a piece of thin cardboard.

5. Paint a branch under the robins. Print pine needles with the edge of some cardboard.

6. When the paint is dry, use a felt-tip pen to add a beak and an eye to each robin.

ISBN 0-439-23310-0

Copyright © 1999, 1998, 1997, 1996, 1995 by Usborne Publishing Limited. All rights reserved. Published by Scholastic Inc., 555 Broadway, New York, NY 10012, by arrangement with Usborne Publishing Ltd. The name Usborne and the device are trademarks of Usborne Publishing Ltd. SCHOLASTIC and associated logos are trademarks and/or registered trademarks of Scholastic Inc.

12 11 10 9 8 7 6 5 4 3 2 1   0 1 2 3 4 5/0

Printed in the U.S.A.   14
* First Scholastic printing, October 2000